Fix a Truck

by Jessica Evans
illustrated by Meryl Henderson

Core Decodable 38

Mc
Graw
Hill
Education

Bothell, WA • Chicago, IL • Columbus, OH • New York, NY

MHEonline.com

Copyright © 2015 McGraw-Hill Education

All rights reserved. No part of this publication may be reproduced or distributed in any form or by any means, or stored in a database or retrieval system, without the prior written consent of McGraw-Hill Education, including, but not limited to, network storage or transmission, or broadcast for distance learning.

Send all inquiries to:
McGraw-Hill Education
8787 Orion Place
Columbus, OH 43240

ISBN: 978-0-02-132932-8
MHID: 0-02-132932-X

Printed in the United States of America.

1 2 3 4 5 6 7 8 9 DOC 20 19 18 17 16 15 14

A red truck had a flat.
It was stuck.

Can the men fix it?

The men pumped a jack.
The truck did not budge!

The truck was filled up.

The men lifted a big box.
The men set it down.

Did it help?
It did not!

The men grabbed fabric.

The truck did not budge!

Next the men lifted six bells.
The men dumped six bells.

The truck still did not budge.

A big man picked up a red pen.

The truck budged!

The men fixed the truck.

15

The men set stuff back in the truck.